For the Living and the Dead

The story of Sheffield General Cemetery

Jo Meredith and Sue Turner

Sheffield General Cemetery Trust

Acknowledgements

This publication was supported by the Heritage Lottery Fund Parks for People project, administered through Sheffield City Council and by Sheffield General Cemetery Trust. Sheffield General Cemetery Trust gratefully acknowledges the Sheffield City Council Archive and the Local Studies service for their ongoing support.

The authors would like to thank all those at the Trust who contributed their time and expertise, particularly for the support of Joseph Batchelor, Shirley Baxter, Helen Brown, Adrian Hallam, Jean Lees, Andrew Littlewood, Marcin Nikoniuk and Cathy Spence. Special mention must also be made of Jane Horton who in 2001 produced the first published history of the Cemetery entitled "Remote and Undisturbed". It was revised by many volunteers at the Trust over the years as change occurred and new information came to light, but the book remained as the source and inspiration for much of the content of this new publication.

Burial research is ongoing. The information presented here is, to the best of our knowledge, correct at the time of publication. We welcome new information and comments: sgct@gencem.org.

Printed by Mensa, 323 Abbeydale Road, Sheffield, S7 1FS
ISBN 9781 739080860
Copyright Sheffield General Cemetery Trust 2023
Published by the Sheffield General Cemetery Trust 2023
Cover Illustration: Courtesy of Jane Horton, 2023

The cemetery is indisputably one of the most beautiful establishments of its kind in the kingdom, and though some of its chief attractions are attributable to the situation, it is much indebted to the skill and taste of the architect, Mr S Worth, who has made it a delightful spot for the perambulations of the living, and a safe depository for the dead.

Gazetteer and General Directory of Sheffield, William White, 1837

Contents

SHEFFIELD GENERAL CEMETERY

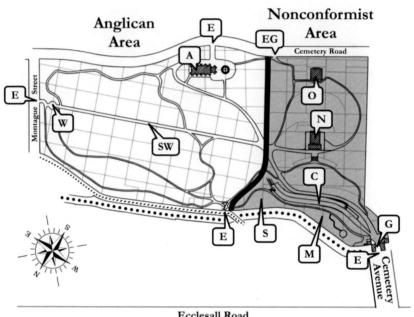

Anglican Area
Nonconformist Area

▬ Dissenters' Wall	⁄⁄⁄⁄⁄ Stalker Walk
A Anglican Chapel	•••• Porter Brook
N Nonconformist Chapel (Samuel Worth Chapel)	**E** Entrance
G Gatehouse	**EG** Egyptian Gate
O Old Cemetery Office	**W** War Memorial
SW Sandford's Walk	**S** Stone Spiral
C Catacombs	**M** Memorial Garden

Introduction

Sheffield General Cemetery can still be described as it was nearly two centuries ago[1] as a delightful spot for both the living and the dead. Between 1836 and 1978 there were nearly 86,500 burials but today the site is enjoyed as a popular heritage park. It remains as a green oasis within the western suburbs, sandwiched between the residential streets of Sharrow and close to the busy commercial route of Ecclesall Road. Its carriageways and paths, originally designed for quiet contemplation, are now equally used by local people walking their dogs or going to the shops; half of the thirteen-acre site has been cleared of gravestones and is a grassy parkland used for picnics, exercise and play. In marked contrast, the older part presents a jumble of monuments and graves, in places overgrown with brambles and trees – a haven for wildlife and for people seeking a moment of calm. People love the Cemetery, whether as a place to meet, walk and talk, as a reminder of the city's history or as the resting place of their ancestors and a resource for family history.

Sheffield's General Cemetery is one of the city's finest historic assets and contains ten listed buildings and monuments at Grade II or above. The site also has a significant place in the history of parks in Britain as, along with the work of the original designer, Samuel Worth, it used the skills of one of the great park designers of the nineteenth century, Robert Marnock. A designated Conservation Area, in 1998 it was added to the National Register of Historic Parks and Gardens as a Grade II site and upgraded to Grade II* status in 2009.

It is also one of the country's earliest cemeteries and has an important place in the history of cemetery design nationally and internationally. Samuel Worth's use of the Egyptian style for the Cemetery buildings in

Sheffield became fashionable in Victorian cemetery design throughout Britain. However, in spite of the influence of its design and style, the Cemetery experienced mixed fortunes in the later nineteenth and the twentieth centuries. Economic success and disaster, pristine maintenance and benign neglect all feature in its history.

People power would save the day when The Friends of the General Cemetery was set up in 1989 to save the site from neglect and to restore key areas, buildings and monuments. The Friends began the first phase of this work with the Gatehouse restoration project, started in the late 1990s and completed in 2004. The renovation and maintenance activities were then taken over by Sheffield General Cemetery Trust and they worked with Sheffield City Council to source income enabling the renovation of the Nonconformist Chapel which reopened in 2015 as the Samuel Worth Chapel. A major grant from the Parks for People programme with additional funding from Sheffield City Council was awarded to enable conservation work to the site's paths and structures to be completed in 2023. Sheffield General Cemetery Trust continue to work with Sheffield City Council to ensure that the Cemetery is cared for and can be used by everyone for educational and recreational purposes.

The Story of Sheffield General Cemetery

Public Health Concerns

The population of England doubled during the first half of the nineteenth century, from nine million in 1801 to eighteen million by 1851. England also became predominantly urban with large numbers of people moving from the countryside to the town so that by 1851, 54 per cent of the population lived in towns compared to 20 per cent in 1801.

Growth was concentrated in urban areas particularly in the Northern and Midland industrial centres of Manchester, Leeds and Birmingham but while new and splendid factories were built, the homes for the working population were often cramped and unsanitary. There were frequent outbreaks of disease including cholera, typhus, typhoid and influenza which, being easily transmitted, spread rapidly. This, along with an increase in industrial and domestic accidents, put enormous pressure on existing burial grounds, usually churchyards, leading to the need for a "Burial Revolution" to follow in the footsteps of the industrial one.

Sheffield's population increase was particularly dramatic as the number of people here trebled, rising from 45,758 in 1801 to 135,310 by 1851. As Sheffield grew so did the problem of where to bury the dead. Churchyards were full to bursting - health hazards in themselves. Several epidemics had swept the town in the early 1830s, and lack of burial space by the mid-1830s was at crisis point. An article from *The Sheffield Independent* in March 1834 stated that: "The very inadequate Provision which is made in Sheffield for the burial of the Dead, has for a long time engaged the public attention". Concern was growing nationally for organised sanitary reform. Southwood Smith, recognised as the father of the modern public health system, was supported by Charles Dickens and many other leading figures in campaigning to eradicate filth and disease. The negative publicity over the poor state of the town's burials and the dangers to the health of Sheffield residents ensured that something was done.

The Royal Commission on the Health of Towns was set up in 1843 and as a result, the Public Health Act of 1848 was passed which recommended that local authorities manage sewers, drainage, burial grounds and public baths. The Commission received reports on fifty different towns, including one on Sheffield by James Smith. His report stated:

> Complaints are made of the offensive nature of the interments within the town. One churchyard in the middle of the town is peculiarly offensive. It is very much crowded with bodies and as the soil is considerably above the level of the surrounding street, the exudation of putrid liquid from the soil is visible to the eye and offensive to the smell. The soil, being of a tenacious clay, the decay of the bodies is slow; and where graves are opened the skeletons are often found still articulated and their exhumation is most offensive to the inhabitants residing within sight of the burial ground.

That this situation still existed several years after the opening of the General Cemetery underlines the appalling situation that must have existed to prompt its establishment in the first place. Smith then went on to praise the General Cemetery Company's undertaking thus:

> A cemetery has just been established at some distance in the country by a Joint Stock Company, under good regulations. It is

beginning to be resorted to and it is hoped that the bulk of the interments will hereafter be made in this or some other similar place; for whether we consider the health and comfort of the inhabitants, or the softer feelings of the relatives of the dead, or generally, feelings of public decency, we must approve of the arrangement of having burial places in a remote and undisturbed locality.

Cramped and insanitary conditions were not the only cause for concern. At the beginning of the nineteenth century body snatching was a constant threat which prompted the introduction of the Anatomy Act in 1832 to try to control this gruesome trade. The growth of medical science and the increase in the number of Anatomy Schools - Sheffield had two - meant that there were insufficient bodies from legitimate sources available for dissection. As a result, newly buried bodies were sometimes stolen to be sold for dissection. This was a lucrative practice as fresh corpses could be sold for more than the yearly income of the average working man. Boundary walls and gates in the new cemeteries of the nineteenth century reflected the need for security, in contrast to the open and hence vulnerable nature of most existing churchyards where body snatching was easy. The Company Minutes from that period show that security guards were employed and the high wall around the Cemetery was a response to the need for protection from body snatchers.

Early Nonconformist Years

Another significant element which contributed to the need for new burial spaces was the rise of the Nonconformist movement. Prominent Nonconformists in Sheffield included many of the rising industrialists and professional men of the period - people who were used to getting things done. Their success is exemplified by the figure of Sheffield's greatest steel baron, Mark Firth, who was buried in the Cemetery.

Industrialisation had provided opportunities which led to the emergence of new professions - surveyors, architects, shopkeepers, bankers, engineers and designers. These people earned more money than labourers and had different social values. Many of them identified with the strong dissenting tradition in Sheffield's religion and politics which allowed them to assert their independence from the established gentry who were more likely to be Anglican and Conservative. Nonconformists and Dissenters[2] were affected and incensed by the attitudes of The Established Church - the Church of England - which could either deny burial to Nonconformists or insist on them engaging in rites from which they were consciously dissenting. The growing reaction of such groups including Methodists, Baptists and many more against the monopoly of the Established Church acted as a real catalyst for change. To address these problems whilst also creating a new business opportunity, a group of Sheffield Nonconformists formed the General Cemetery Company.

The greatest influence on English cemetery design at this time came from France where problems of overcrowding in urban churchyards and the vast numbers of dead bodies, often left rotting in the streets during the period of the French Revolution, had already prompted drastic measures. In 1784 the main burial grounds of central Paris were closed and in the following two years all bones and remains were cleared and placed in catacombs. Cemeteries were then established in three areas on the outskirts of the city; the largest of the three was the Père-Lachaise Cemetery where the first burial took place in 1804. That cemetery had aspects that were to influence developments in England, and specifically Sheffield, in terms of design and economics. Interestingly a model of Père-Lachaise Cemetery toured round England and was exhibited in the Sheffield Assembly Rooms in 1829.

Cemeteries, that is burial grounds separate from a church building, had been established throughout Europe in the eighteenth century but they tended to be small scale and were generally linked to a particular church. It was not until the nineteenth century that the large scale, commercially run cemeteries appeared. In 1819 the first cemetery company was formed in England. This was the Rosary Cemetery in Norwich which opened as a direct result of a local vicar's refusal to bury a child who had been baptised in the Methodist Chapel and not the Anglican Church. From then, until the establishment of local burial boards in 1852, commercial cemeteries were created in many cities; notable examples include the Liverpool Necropolis (1825), Glasgow Necropolis (1832), Kensal Green in London (1832), Key Hill Cemetery in Birmingham (1834) and London's Highgate Cemetery (1839).

Commercial Burials in a Classical Landscape

The concept of commercial burial was relatively new when the General Cemetery was first established. In 1834, at the first meeting of subscribers, some of Sheffield's most influential citizens gathered at the Cutlers' Hall to consider the prospect of a new burial ground "at some distance in the countryside". They were prompted, no doubt, by the 1832 outbreak of cholera in Sheffield. Over 400 people died in the town within such a short space of time that the only place they could be buried was in a special cholera burial ground now marked by the Cholera Monument[3]. Nearly every one of the subscribers at that first meeting was from the professional and middle classes, with merchants, manufacturers, doctors, surgeons and bankers among them. Four of the original subscribers including **Thomas Asline Ward** (1781-1871), diarist and founder of the Literary and Philosophical Society, had been Master Cutlers of Sheffield. Asline Ward was undoubtedly the most notable of the group and the prime mover of the General Cemetery development. He was also the recently appointed Chairman of the newly formed Board of Health, one of the first in the country, set up in Sheffield in 1831 to minimise the spread of infection.

Nine acres of land on which the General Cemetery was to be built were bought for £1,900 from Henry Wilson of Westbrook, a snuff manufacturer, whose snuff mill was a few hundred yards further along the Porter Valley. It was a relatively cheap piece of land being on a steep, northerly slope and hence less attractive for residential development. It was, however, quite close to where the newly prosperous manufacturing and professional classes were establishing their homes. Only five acres of the land purchased were to be enclosed at first as that was considered to be sufficient for several generations of burials. However, this was to be no ordinary burial ground and the requirements of the shareholders were very demanding. Henry Wilson's snuff mill was situated in an idyllic spot and he was concerned to ensure that the design of the Cemetery would not detract from the beauty of the Porter Valley. Two drafts of a conveyance document were produced detailing the proposals for the site. These conveyance documents allowed for the transfer of four fields in this rural area to the Cemetery Company and the diversion of the River Porter to make a cleaner line at the base of the site.

The design of the Cemetery was put out to competition and won by **Samuel Worth** (1799-1870). Worth was a local architect who had already worked on public buildings in Sheffield including the Cutlers' Hall. According to the Cemetery Company Minutes the project he was to undertake was described by the company shareholders as "an undertaking of no ordinary magnitude – very difficult and expensive to excavate". Worth's plans were ambitious, taking full advantage of the steeply sloping site which gave him a great opportunity to demonstrate his architectural and landscape design skills. He used a style combining Classical and Egyptian elements which subsequently became popular in other Victorian cemeteries including Highgate in London which opened in 1839. In the *Sheffield Independent* of 1 August 1834 Samuel Worth's office advertised tenders for work on the new cemetery for the erection of a bridge and walling, and for sundry excavations required for a proposed diversion of the course of

Thomas Asline Ward,
Master Cutler 1816

15

the Porter Brook, and the forming of a Carriage Entrance Road. Worth's Cemetery design was also significant because of its likely influence on the work of **John Claudius Loudon** (1783-1843).

Loudon, who was a Scottish botanist and well known as a champion of the parks movement in nineteenth-century England, became hugely influential with his strong views about the nature and layout of cemeteries. The publication in 1843 of *"On the Laying Out Planting and Managing of Cemeteries"* represented a landmark for the cemetery movement. In it Loudon dealt with every aspect of cemetery design. He expressed strong views on the style that should be employed and emphasised how cemeteries could offer instruction by example in many fields of study, including sculpture and botany. Loudon promoted the use of evergreen trees and shrubs, many recently introduced from abroad, and suggested that cemeteries could be made into arboreta or botanical gardens. Loudon had connections with Sheffield that may have influenced some of the information in his book, and he and his wife visited the General Cemetery in May 1839. His book proposes a plan for the laying out of a cemetery on a hilly site. While it does not acknowledge Sheffield General Cemetery as its source, it can be no coincidence that the plan is almost a replica of the General Cemetery layout. In the event Loudon went on to execute this design for Southampton Cemetery in 1843. Loudon's "garden cemetery" style came to be used in all new cemeteries until more utilitarian styles prevailed in later years.

Samuel Worth also considered the Cemetery's place in the broad landscape of the Porter Valley. The Nonconformist Chapel at the centre of the five-acre Cemetery was in a direct line of sight across the valley to the "handsome Ionic edifice" of the grand residence, The Mount, built and designed in 1833 by the upcoming architect **William**

Flockton (1804-1864). The Sheffield Botanical and Horticultural Society was formed in June 1833 with the intention of creating a botanical garden to promote healthy recreation and self-improvement. The Botanical Gardens, opened in 1836 shortly after the General Cemetery, were laid out on 18 acres of south facing farmland on the northern slopes of the Porter Valley. Admission to the Botanical Gardens was limited to shareholders and annual subscribers except for four Gala days per year when the gates opened to the general public. These two new garden areas on either side of the river made the Porter Valley a desirable place for Sheffielders to spend time, away from town centre filth and pollution, but within easy walking distance.

By 1838 the grand porticoed front elevation, also designed by Flockton, of the Wesleyan Proprietary College, now King Edward VII School, would also be visible. Newly prominent on the south facing slopes of the valley from Broomhill down to Broomhall were the classical styled homes, schools and churches of Sheffield's emerging middle class. Worth lived in an Ionic Greek villa - West Mount on Glossop Road – which he had designed for himself, and he would have seen his creation from the principal rooms of his new home. For this brief period in the nineteenth century before the suburbs grew, the Porter Valley was transformed into an Arcadian vision of a classical landscape.

Thomas Asline Ward had also been one of the promoters of the Botanical Gardens and it is easy to see how interconnected the different people and the landscape developments were at this time. **Robert Marnock** (1800-1889) the garden design and horticulturalist who became the first curator of the Botanical Gardens, acted as consultant in this first phase of the Cemetery's life.

In 1836 *The Sheffield Mercury* reported the opening of "the new cemetery, a pleasant grassy lawn by the side of the River Porter thickly shadowed over by Oak, Ash and Elder" and in the same year *The Sheffield Independent* referred to "the crowds of people who are in the habit of visiting this very attractive and interesting place".

William White's *Gazetteer and General Directory of Sheffield*, 1837 stated that:

> the cemetery is indisputably one of the most beautiful establishments of its kind in the kingdom, and though some of its chief attractions are attributable to the situation, it is much indebted to the skill and taste of the architect, Mr S Worth, who has made it a delightful spot for the perambulations of the living, and a safe depository for the dead.

The main approach from the Manchester Turnpike Road, now Ecclesall Road, was along Cemetery Avenue. At the junction of the roads two obelisks were erected and remained in place until 1926. Cemetery Avenue was lined with lime trees and a low wall flanked either side of the road. The approach was an integral part of the landscape plan. In fact, an earlier Worth plan for this entrance avenue was much more dramatic. This had allowed for a gently winding pathway, starting at ground level, and building up gradually so that at the point it reached and crossed the River Porter, the path was raised 12 feet in the air with parapets on either side. Whatever the reason for the early plan being abandoned, the fact that it was drawn up at all demonstrates how grand a vision Samuel Worth had for the site, which apart from this most flamboyant part of the proposal, was executed according to his plan.

Obelisks belonging to the General Cemetery, Cemetery Avenue

The First Cemetery Buildings

The **Gatehouse** (listed Grade II*) at the main entrance was important in establishing the first impression of the Cemetery which would have been clearly visible rising in tiers up the hillside beyond. The main gateway, side lodges and supporting bridge were designed in a classical revival style and built of blocks of Millstone Grit.

The Gatehouse

The building sits on a substantial wide bridge that spans the Porter Brook. This location can be interpreted as a classical reference to reaching the Elysian Fields - that is the afterlife - after crossing the River Styx, or as a Judeo/Christian one of crossing the River Jordan to reach the Promised Land. Elaborate wrought iron gates were installed at the Gatehouse in the late Victorian period. The design for the gates was ingenious - they did not swing open but slid back into spaces built into the Gatehouse thus allowing the widest possible access into the grounds. These gates survived into the 1970s when they were replaced. The Gatehouse was not just the entrance to the Cemetery but provided accommodation for Cemetery workers such as the Sexton and the Gravedigger.

The original landscape plan made much use of the dramatic hillside setting and the **Catacombs** (listed Grade II) were incorporated into the steeply sloping site. The main serpentine path sweeps up the hill in a giant reversed "S" shape. This is emphasised by the two curving tiers of the Catacombs close to the Gatehouse that followed the line of the main path. The Catacomb doorways were designed to have iron gates at the entrances once they became occupied. Some gates were ordered but there is no evidence that they were installed. Below the Catacombs, close to the point at which the steps from the Catacombs descend to the Porter Brook, a footbridge was provided leading over the river to what is now Stalker Lees Road.

The Catacombs, 2004

The Catacombs did not prove popular and very few were sold. This may have been a surprise to the Company Directors who were probably aware of the success of the catacombs in Père-Lachaise Cemetery in Paris. This lack of popularity may have been in part due to their price. A private vault or crypt in the Catacombs cost £5.5.0. whereas land for a private grave could be purchased for £1.10.0. In practice most burials that took place in the Cemetery were not those of the wealthy Dissenters the Company was hoping for. It is also possible that Sheffield people had a reluctance to adopt above-ground burials which were more acceptable in other countries. Whatever the reason the Catacombs were expensive to create and unfortunately for the General Cemetery Company were not profitable, although in later years they were used for public burials. However not only did they help to unify a stunning landscape they were essential to its survival, as they also buttressed the steeply rising hillside.

Halfway up the hill the main path sweeps back to the **Chapel** (listed Grade II*) which sits squarely in the middle of the site and was the centrepiece of the original Cemetery plan. The design of the Nonconformist Chapel was described in the *Pevsner Architectural Guide* as "Egypto-Greek" and again constructed using Derbyshire Millstone Grit. It was built to a great depth: the subterranean part of the structure being equal in depth to the height of the building above ground. A range of stone-faced catacombs to the rear of the Chapel acted as a retaining wall to the surrounding burial ground and provided access via a sunken driveway to the deep vaults beneath the Chapel. Facing the vaults was a perpendicular rock face, creating a dell, which was filled in towards the end of the nineteenth century.

Artist's impression of the rear
of the Nonconformist Chapel

The front of the Chapel has a portico with substantial fluted Doric columns beneath it. Under the portico there is a large Egyptian style doorway. Above the door there is a sculpted relief panel of a dove representing the Holy Spirit descending. Each side elevation has four simply framed Egyptian windows with octagonal iron fretwork.

The Nonconformist Chapel

There was initially an intention to paint the inside of the Chapel although the architect was informed that the committee would not "pay any further expense of colouring". The Chapel was principally designed for funerals but after it was built Sunday services were held there. Evening services, however, were soon discontinued owing to the severe coldness of the building.

The main path in front of the Chapel curves up to the west towards the **Cemetery Office** (listed Grade II) and the southerly entrance to the site. Clearly showing Samuel Worth's eclectic style the square Office building has pairs of long, sloping, simply framed windows on each side, shaped like the doorways in Egyptian tombs, and Classical style pillars on either side of the door.

The Cemetery Office, later renamed Montague House

The Egyptian Gate

Close to the Office there is the **Egyptian Gate** (listed Grade II*). This unusual entrance was designed in an Egyptian style with iron rail gates richly ornamented with symbolic references. The ouroboros (snakes eating their tails) in the centre of each gate is an ancient symbol of immortality and rebirth. There are also fasces, an Etruscan and later Roman symbol of magisterial power and sometimes of unity, and the winged orb, a symbol of Egyptian mythology. This latter symbol appears above the gate and was commonly found over the entrances to ancient Egyptian tombs and symbolises the triumph of day over night, light over dark and good over evil. The design also echoes the symbol of the Holy Spirit descending in the form of a dove, which can be seen above the entrance to the Nonconformist Chapel.

Worth was also tasked with the laying out of the grounds which began in March 1836, possibly according to designs by Robert Marnock. On 28 August 1837 Marnock was thanked "for his services in inspecting the laying out and planting of the Cemetery; and that he be requested to accept a donation of £5 as an acknowledgement thereof".[4]

By retaining individual trees on the site, including an ancient oak which stood immediately to the north-west of the Chapel, together with fragments of earlier field boundaries, Worth skilfully created an idealised, naturalistic landscape which was widely applauded. The *Sheffield Mercury* of 27 August 1836 referred to the Cemetery as a "place peculiarly dedicated to the dead, and, at the same time, a beautiful resort for the living" noting that "judgement and taste are equally conspicuous." On passing the Lodge "a broad gravel walk leads to the lower range of vaults, in the front of which there is a pleasant grassy lawn by the side of the River Porter, which is here thickly shadowed over with oak, ash, and elder". After J C Loudan visited the Cemetery in 1839 he noted in *The Gardener's Magazine* that the winding walks are "judiciously interspersed with trees and shrubs by Mr Marnock".

Mixed Fortunes

From the first burial in May 1836 of Mary Ann Fish, the wife of a bookkeeper, who died of consumption at the age of 24, the General Cemetery Company had mixed fortunes. For the first few years the annual meetings of Directors often took place in the Cutlers' Hall - an indication of the status of the Cemetery Company in Sheffield society. Its starting point had been ambitious and it is clear that the Company struggled as a result of the excessive cost of achieving its vision for the site. The year before opening the Directors had stated that "the whole undertaking has acquired a magnitude and incurred difficulties, which far surpass what was first, contemplated".[5] However, the original landscape layout had an air of confidence about it as the amount of money spent on the development demonstrates: the whole amount expended being around £13,000, a very significant sum in the 1830s.

Lithograph from T C Hofland's painting of Sheffield General Cemetery

In order to promote the Cemetery, the Company commissioned Thomas Christoper Hofland (1777-1843) to produce a painting and engravings.

The Directors were optimistic about the Cemetery's appeal and in 1837 reported to their subscribers in glowing terms:

> Situated beyond the precinct of the town; in its scenery, picturesque and enchanting, exhibiting amidst the stillness which befits the repose of the dead, so many forms of life to remind the spectator rather of the future resurrection than of the temporary dissolution of the body......The Sheffield General Cemetery may be expected, ere long, to receive, as a place of burial, a very extensive share of public patronage, as it must indubitably obtain a high rank in public esteem.
>
> *Sheffield General Cemetery Directors' Report, 1837*

By the next year however, the Directors were commenting on the unparalleled depression in the state of trade that Sheffield, as well as other parts of the country, was suffering: "The pecuniary resources of the bulk of the population have been nearly or altogether exhausted; which persons of every class of society have experienced a share of the common difficulties always attendant on a season of commercial suffering". The earlier table of charges set by the Company was substantially reduced and thousands of advertising flyers were printed and delivered to houses in the town. The Directors negotiated with the Guardians of the Poor for the Sheffield Union workhouse for the price of four shillings and six pence for the interment of each pauper in a bid to boost income. Plainly the shareholders were not going to get as good an immediate return on their investment as they had been led to expect.

On completion of the Cemetery one of the first issues that engaged the Directors were the gravestones that were to be erected. In July 1837 the position of "Stone-mason, letter-cutter etc" was advertised and a stone yard with a stonemason's workshop was built in the Cemetery. The taking of the stonework in-house was guided by "the example afforded in other towns, by the urgent necessity of the case, and by conviction of the great importance of pursuing such plans as will secure the richest display of elegance, propriety, and taste in the varied memorials which affection may place above the ashes of departed friends". It was also another business opportunity.

From the opening of the Cemetery in May 1836 it took six years to sell the first 1,000 plots. By 1843 it was thought that the Cemetery was "slowly but surely, increasing in public estimation notwithstanding the prejudices which deprive it of the support of a numerous and influential class". Security issues and incidences of vandalism did not help the growth of the Cemetery nor did the toll charged for funeral vehicles at the Ecclesall Road turnpike.

Better off people, for the most part, were still not choosing the General Cemetery as their final resting place. The Directors considered why it was not more popular when its picturesque and architectural attractions were so great and concluded that objections existed which were not confined to the operative classes, but also to the wealthy and opulent. In 1841 the Company first recorded its concerns about the prevailing prejudice against the Cemetery which they believed to be because it had not been consecrated according to the rites of the Established Church. The Company realised that action had to be taken if it was to succeed as a commercial venture.

The Anglican Consecrated Ground

In order to increase the number of burials and the range of people to whom the site would appeal there was a flurry of activity in the late 1840s. The Company bought extra land to add to the remaining unused acres from the original purchase with the intention of establishing a new area of consecrated ground. A low wall from the top to the bottom of the site, the perimeter wall of the original Cemetery, now became the division between the Nonconformist and the Anglican sections of the burial ground and was known as the **Dissenters' Wall.**

Dissenters' Wall

William Flockton was chosen to develop a Chapel within the new Anglican area of the Cemetery. Flockton was the son of a carpenter and builder, Thomas Flockton, but was ambitious to do more than simply follow in the family firm. In the early 1830s he conceived a scheme to finance and build The Mount – a grand terrace of eight houses built in a bold classical style prominently sited on the hillside of Broomhill. Originally referred to as "Flockton's Folly" it soon became a financial success and acted as great publicity for the young architect. The great and good of Sheffield including James Montgomery and George Wostenholm were some of the original tenants. The Wesley Proprietary Grammar School, later to be called Wesley College and then King Edward VII School, opened in 1838 and another impressive classical façade by Flockton adorned the slopes of the as yet undeveloped Broomhill. In later years Flockton went on to design the Ecclesall Union Workhouse and many large houses such as Kenwood in Nether Edge for George Wostenholm, working there with Marnock who designed the grounds. Wostenholm who went on to become Master Cutler in 1856, was on the General Cemetery Company's committee. Flockton's son, Thomas, also became an architect and the resultant companies of Flockton, Lee and Flockton and later Flockton and Gibbs were responsible for many of Sheffield's nineteenth century churches, schools and town centre buildings.

Flockton's design for the **Anglican Chapel** (listed Grade II) was a confident neo-Gothic work whose detailed exterior contrasted with the simplicity of the neoclassical Nonconformist Chapel.

The juxtaposition of the two opposing building styles was a feature that made the Cemetery unique. The Chapel was constructed using two different sandstones. The corner stones were cut from Millstone Grit but the main walls were constructed using the local Coal Measures sandstone. The spire of the Anglican Chapel was deliberately out of proportion to the rest of the building and so was visible from a considerable distance. Clearly Flockton played up its size to give it prominence in the landscape. *White's Directory* for 1849 refers to the construction of "a handsome church in the decorated style of early English architecture, with a lofty tower and spire" and how "the chapel .... and the church, standing near the crown of the acclivity, form conspicuous objects in the beautiful vale of the Porter, on the opposite side of which are the Botanical Gardens and many handsome villas".

The first stone of the Anglican Chapel was laid by the Reverend Dr Sutton, Vicar of Sheffield, on 8 May 1848 and the ground was consecrated by his Grace the Archbishop of York on 27 June 1850 during a service at which a special hymn was sung, composed by the poet James Montgomery (1771-1854).

Engraving of the Sheffield New Cemetery Church, c1848

The General Cemetery Company commissioned Robert Marnock to design the layout of the new grounds. Marnock by this time had a well-established national reputation. In 1840 he won a competition to design the garden of the Royal Botanic Society in London's Regent Park where he worked until 1862. He designed parks and gardens throughout England and the Continent before returning to Sheffield where he carried out work on some large private estates and gardens.

In 1873 Marnock was commissioned by Sheffield Council to lay out Weston Park, Sheffield's first public park, which opened in 1875.

Marnock submitted a plan for the consecrated area of the Cemetery in 1850 and the planting and supply of shrubs was tendered for. By August 1850 the Company reports were stating "the planting may now be seen to advantage... the beauty of its scenery, when taken in connection with the adjacent Botanical Gardens may be considered unrivalled in this or any other country".

Once the Anglican ground was open, trade picked up quickly. The period from 1850 to 1890 was a busy one and the Cemetery finally became profitable.

1851 Ordnance Survey map showing the curved pathways newly laid out by Marnock

Sheffield General Cemetery,

INCORPORATED BY STATUTE, 9 & 10 VIC., C. 284.

—o—

CHARGES, &c.

Public and Common Graves.

	£.	s.	d.
Single Interment, in Public Graves.			
For a Still-born Child............................	0	2	0
For Children under six years of age..............	0	4	6
For Adults, and for Children above six years of age	0	6	0
Single Interment, in Common Grave	0	10	0
In select situations.................	0	15	0

N.B. Interments in this section do not confer any Right or Property in the grave.

Private Graves.

Land for a Private Grave in some parts of the Cemetery ..	1	0	0
For each Interment therein, including digging same seven feet deep	0	7	0
Land for a Private Grave, in other parts of the Cemetery, according to situation, £1 10s. and upwards			
For each Interment therein, including digging same seven feet deep..	0	12	6

N.B. An Extra Charge is made for digging Graves more than seven feet deep.

Vaults, Catacombs, &c.

A Private Vault, or Crypt, for a single interment..........	5	5	0
A Family Vault, varying in size and situation, £10 and upwards.			
The first interment in a Vault or Catacomb	1	0	0
For each subsequent interment therein	1	10	0

Extra Charges.

For every Interment in a Private or Public Grave, in the Consecrated part of the Cemetery (being the compensation fee to the Incumbent of the parish)	0	1	6
For ditto in a Vault, or Brick Grave	0	5	0
For Tolling the Bell, when required......................	0	1	0
Interments in Private Graves, before three o'clock........	0	10	0
Ditto in Vaults or Catacombs	0	15	0
For removing and replacing Gravestones	0	2	6
For maintaing plants over graves (if required) per annum..	0	5	0
For ditto in perpetuity	5	0	0

—o—

GRAVESTONES, MONUMENTS, AND TOMBS

Are Furnished and Lettered by the Company, at moderate charges, at their Stone Works, Sheffield Cemetery. A Stock of Headstones, Gravestones, &c., constantly on hand.

REGULATIONS.

All Dues and Fees to be paid to the Secretary before the grave, vault, &c., be opened.

Persons having interments may avail themselves of the services of their own minister, on giving notice at the time of ordering the interment.

Flat Gravestones *only* will be allowed on every alternate row of graves, in order to allow access to the intermediate graves.

Palisading will be allowed *only in some* parts of the Cemetery, and a fee of One Guinea will be charged for admission.

Monumental Tablets may be erected in the Church, on payment of a fee of Five Guineas when such tablet does not occupy more space than ten superficial feet; and tablets occupying above ten, and not more than twenty superficial feet, on payment of a fee of Ten Guineas; and for every additional foot above twenty feet, a fee of Half-a-Guinea per foot will be charged.

All Monuments, Gravestones, Vaults, and places of burial, to be kept in repair by the owners, to the satisfaction of the Directors.

☞ *Any further Particulars may be ascertained on enquiry at the Cemetery Lodge, and communications may be addressed to the Secretary of the Company.*

From 1852 through to 1857 there was a sequence of Burial Acts restricting further burials in existing churchyards in towns and regulating cemeteries, which effectively endorsed the commercial innovations of joint stock companies including the General Cemetery Company. The Sheffield Parish Burial Board was established following the 1852 Act and set up its first cemeteries in Sheffield at Darnall and Attercliffe. Both were relatively small, restrained in design and geographically remote from the General Cemetery. Nor were they particularly attractive to the kind of person the General Cemetery sought to attract.

In 1853 the Chaplain of the Anglican Chapel, George Sandford, asked for the privilege of planting beech and lime trees on the walk intersecting the consecrated ground. This avenue became known as Sandford's Walk.

Sandford's Walk

In May 1855 one of the Company's Directors visited the cemeteries at Brompton and Kensal Green in London and discovered that by reducing the size of each plot and having rectilinear rather than serpentine paths, "upwards of one thousand additional Graves would be obtained". This would considerably increase the potential income of the Cemetery and the directors unanimously resolved to incorporate this proposal into the lower half of the consecrated area. The romantic curved lines designed by Marnock were replaced with regimented rows of gravestones. This utilitarian approach, in line with the style of the Burial Board Cemeteries, made space for many more graves. The new configuration of walks is clearly visible on later Ordnance Survey maps.

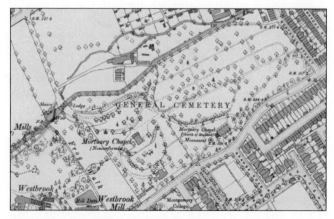

1894 Ordnance Survey map showing the Cemetery with more linear paths

In 1857 Wardsend Cemetery was established on the north side of Sheffield This catered for a wealthier class than the two earlier Burial Board cemeteries and may have taken some trade away from the General Cemetery. In 1861, Burngreave Cemetery was established to the northeast of the town centre which added real competition to the Cemetery. Burngreave Cemetery had two chapels designed by Flockton and it was substantial in size (27 acres) - twice the size of the General Cemetery which now covered 13 acres. However, the population of Sheffield was by now so large at 185,155 that there was plenty of trade to go round.

Disasters and Mishaps

In 1864 the Company's Minutes noted the dreadful calamity of the Sheffield Flood. 66 Flood victims were buried in the Cemetery including 27 unidentified casualties, 16 of them children. Later the body of John Gunson was also buried here. He was the resident engineer who was initially held responsible for the dam burst that caused the Flood but later exonerated from blame. The story of this tragedy was well-documented nationwide thanks to the work of Samuel Harrison who wrote the first account of the Flood and who was also buried in the Cemetery.

From 1863 into the early 1870s the site suffered a few mishaps. Heavy rains led to the River Porter breaking its banks on several occasions. The walls had to be rebuilt more than once and a new river wall was erected in 1871. This was accompanied by the repair of the walk beside the River Porter. This section of the walk was dedicated in 1871 and designated a public road. The problem of flooding at the base of the Cemetery was also to cost the Company significant sums in the future. In 1876 water was supplied to the Lodges at the Gatehouse, 40 years after they were first built, following complaints about offensive matter being allowed to flow into the Porter from this point. No mention appears to have been made of the already dirty water that the inhabitants of the Gatehouse lodges had to take from the river for their daily use.

In 1865 *The Sheffield Daily Telegraph* reported disagreeable mismanagement at the General Cemetery. This referred to a growing battle over vicars' fees which escalated in 1867 to become a court case. The vicars' case rested on the fact that where there were no burial spaces left in graveyards in their parishes, or no graveyards at all, they were still entitled to a fee per body from their district. Of the seven priests involved in the dispute, three had chapel yards and four did not. Payment of such fees threatened to cut into the Company's profit margin.

The Cemetery Minutes show that vandalism is not a recent phenomenon. In August 1838 it was resolved that a "Board be placed at the obelisks, giving notice that a reward of one guinea will be paid upon conviction of the offender, to any person giving information of any individual found injuring trees on the avenue, or committing depredations in the Cemetery". By 1844 entrance was controlled by tickets, "the operation of which has produced that decency and decorum, which ought to prevail near the mansions of the dead". Problems were encountered with residents on the newly built Sharrow Head estate and throughout the 1860s and 1870s there were references to the need to engage more policemen on Sundays.

Between 1870 and 1900 the Cemetery was extremely busy but the site was not being looked after properly and in 1898 the Minutes record that complaints had been received about the state of the grounds. The Company had a limited amount of money available for improvement and this would be reduced if the Cemetery was not considered an attractive option for burial. A report commissioned by the Company suggested that the grounds needed to be better cared for, that graves left unstoned two years after the interment should be repossessed and that a courteous and sympathetic Secretary could do much to remove the bad impression attached to the Cemetery. Appeals were launched encouraging the plot holders, who were the legal owners of the land on which their grave stood, to act more responsibly and care for their plots and more labour was employed to care for the site although the closeness of stones in some areas made this difficult.

Twentieth Century Challenges

Victorian cemeteries were not designed to be easy to look after. They were constructed in a period when labour was cheap, materials plentiful and the general public, especially the upper and middle classes, were prepared to spend a great deal on funerals. From the turn of the twentieth century onwards the Company Minutes document many repairs to the grounds. In 1909 gates were repaired and in 1912 the roofs of the Lodges, Chapel and the Offices were re-slated. Trees were pruned in 1913 and dead ones removed. Sandford's Walk was straightened with a flagged stone path added and in 1913 the path between the Office and the Chapel was turfed over and the Dissenters' Wall built up.

By this time the pressure on space for burials was becoming a problem and in 1916, to free up more grave space, there were plans to remove a large copper beech tree and the Italian garden, an area in front of the Cemetery Office which was used to showcase marble headstones. Surveyors were asked to advise on whether the steep area down the hill from the John Cole monument on the main carriageway could be brought into use. Despite the resulting creation of new spaces for burials, available plots and choice of location was limited.

After the Great War the grand Victorian style of funeral seemed almost distasteful in the face of the terrible numbers of war dead. A combination of this change in attitude, the shortage of burial spaces and a gradual acceptance of cremation as a suitable alternative to burial, caused the Company's income to fall. People were also living longer as health and sanitation improved. At the same time there was an increasing need for maintenance on the site and the costs of labour and materials were growing. The signs were not good and the General Cemetery Company went into decline.

In the 1930s plans for improvements were drawn up, possibly in order to celebrate the Cemetery's centenary. A local plant nursery, Fisher, Son and Sibray submitted planting plans to improve the grounds and electric lighting was installed in the Lodges at the end of 1935. In the centenary year of 1936 changes were proposed to the original landscape layout above the Catacombs: the vault heights were to be increased to footpath level by excavating above the arches, breaking in the arch tops and pulling down the stone walls to the level required to make 36 reinforced concrete vaults. A concrete balustrade was to be built along the length of the top tier. A few months later, before the work was complete, there was extensive subsidence due to heavy rains which caused the collapse of some Catacombs and the carriage road. The contractors Hodkin and Jones implemented work on some of the plan, including the balustrade, along with the restoration work to repair flood damage. A further landslide took place in 1937. The necessary repairs "required much expenditure" (£3,442) and as it was economically impossible to reconstruct the destroyed Catacombs they were converted into small vaults.

The Second World war added directly to the Company's problems. The Cemetery Office, then occupied by the General Manager and his family, was used by a local Air Raid Precautions unit and on the night of the Sheffield Blitz, 12 December 1940, a bomb fell in Cemetery Road damaging the east end of the Anglican Chapel, the boundary wall and several memorials. The Cemetery sustained other bomb damage and the Nonconformist Chapel roof was badly damaged. Throughout the War fees for repairs to bomb damage were documented but the last Minute of the General Cemetery Company in 1949 ominously reads "war damages claim still outstanding".

Church of England Mortuary Chapel, showing air raid damage
12 December 1940

Years of Neglect

In the 1950s the Cemetery Company was still selling burial plots in perpetuity although very few burials were taking place, with an average of about 12 per year. Most of these were burials in existing family plots which had been bought in perpetuity, as was the last burial which took place in 1978. Selling plots in perpetuity of course eventually creates problems for any cemetery with a limited amount of space.

The Cemetery Company offered to sell the General Cemetery to the City but after an examination of the accounts the Corporation decided it was not financially viable and the offer was declined. Besides, by then they had plenty of other cemeteries and crematoria of their own.

By this time the Cemetery was in a very poor state of repair and overrun with rats. In 1954 when Martin Flannery, an MP in the 1960s, was teaching at the Porter Croft School which overlooks the Cemetery; he reported that a child had been badly bitten by a rat and another badly injured by a fall in the Cemetery. He added, "It was so dreadfully overrun and so wild, it was not only an eyesore, but the city had a sense of shame about it"[6].

In 1963 Boden Developments Ltd bought most of the shares of the Cemetery Company intending to use the site for a housing development although they also planned to retain a small area as a memorial garden. This news caused a great deal of local opposition and protests from owners of plots and it rapidly became clear that this development could not go ahead. Boden Developments were informed that a planning application for the site would not succeed. The plan was abandoned and the site became even more derelict, dangerous and overgrown, and more of a liability to its owners.

The Cemetery 1964

The Cemetery 1975

Photographs of the Cemetery taken at this time give a good impression of what the site was like before the clearance and although they provide by no means a complete picture, they illustrate how overcrowded the Anglican part of the Cemetery had become. In general, the monuments on the Anglican side were more uniform than those on the Nonconformist side and certainly the layout had long since diverged from Marnock's romantic scheme to become that of the Burial Board style of compact spaces and straight rows.

Top of the Catacombs 1978

Regeneration and Recovery

In 1974 Sheffield City Council made moves to take over the site with the intention of considering alternative uses. To do this the Cemetery had to be closed by the grant of an Order in Council (Burial Act 1853). However, this process was complicated by the fact that plots had been sold by a Deed of Grant in perpetuity and could therefore be inherited as such.

In 1976 the City Council acted under the Planning Acts to secure urgent maintenance works on the Gatehouse. At the same time Evans Ltd, the parent company for Boden Developments, approached the Council and indicated that they would be willing to transfer the General Cemetery to the City Council free of charge. They suggested that if the Council refused this offer it would be likely that Evans Ltd. would consider the voluntary liquidation of the Cemetery Company as the Cemetery had become too much of a liability. As a result, the Council sought an Act of Parliament to enable them to gain ownership of the land. The Council's plan was to keep the western side of the Cemetery as an example of early Victorian cemetery architecture and for the memorials on the eastern side to be removed and the area grassed over to provide a much-needed green space for the local community. To do this the Council first had to hold a Committee of Enquiry which involved listening to the views of affected people: plot owners, local residents and community groups. Some individuals with family graves objected but the overwhelming opinion was one of wanting to see the site tidied up and kept as an open space with no possibility of any building development. The City Council agreed to take on the conservation of the older Nonconformist area whilst clearing the Anglican side. It also proposed a maintenance programme and some enhancements to the older Cemetery for recreational purposes. This plan of action culminated in an Act of Parliament which was given Royal Assent in 1979.

A programme of work began. Unlike many other cemeteries and church yards cleared in the 1960s and 1970s, the memorials in the Cemetery were first documented so that the information was available to families wishing to find out more about their ancestors. This included transcribing the epitaphs, names and dates on all the gravestones, including those in the Nonconformist area which were not due for removal. The information gathered is now held in Sheffield Archives and by the Sheffield General Cemetery Trust.

The Council undertook some emergency repairs. Gaps in the perimeter walls were made good and some of the dangerous structures, particularly the Catacombs, were made safe.

The Council advertised their plan to clear the graves and plot owners were offered help with exhumations and reburials elsewhere. Since there were very few requests for this, most of the bodies were left in position. In 1980, despite opposition from some relatives and grave owners, the bulldozers moved in and the removal of 7,800 gravestones went ahead. Some gravestones in the Anglican area of the Cemetery were left in place and others re-sited so as to save a representative selection of the monuments and their designs. The gravestones removed were either crushed and used as hardcore for paths, or cut and used as edging for paths, or buried on site. In 1986 the Cemetery was designated a Conservation Area.

The Company Office was saved from dereliction in 1987 when a local firm of architects bought the listed building, restored it for use as their own Offices and renamed it Montague House. It later changed its use to be occupied by a children's nursery. In contrast, the Anglican

Chapel has stood derelict for many years. In 1991 a local businessman took out a long lease on the Chapel and submitted a planning application for its conversion into offices. Despite objections, approval was given. This allowed car parking within the Cemetery and the creation of a new access into the site. The development never took place and permission for the project lapsed. Subsequent applications were made to convert the building into residential use and permission was granted in 2012.

The open space after the clearance of the headstones

In 1989 the Friends of the General Cemetery (FOGC) was established out of concern for the state of the Cemetery. The group was set up by several concerned local residents following a well-attended public meeting. The aims of the group were to raise awareness about the value of the site, to encourage its use for educational purposes and to protect and ultimately to restore and regenerate the site. FOGC became a registered charity in 1990.

The Friends, led by Jane Horton and supported by Julia Duggleby, immediately began to research the history of the site, provide information and conduct tours every month. Special interest talks on geology, flora and fauna, the environment and local history were given to the universities, local schools and to any group that wished to use the Cemetery as a resource. The numbers attending these tours grew over the years as did the Friends' knowledge and understanding of the site.

In 1992 the Council undertook some maintenance on the site and in the mid-1990s FOGC received several grants and donations for restoration work. This enabled the restoration of the Egyptian Gate and Mark Firth's memorial railings and maintenance work on footpaths and planting. FOGC established regular working arrangements with Sheffield Conservation Volunteers and other groups which continue under the Cemetery Trust. A Health and Safety Review led to the removal of some of the historic landscape elements of the Cemetery, including the removal of the retaining wall behind the Nonconformist Chapel. Large areas of the Cemetery were fenced off with wooden paling to protect the public from danger and to protect the Council from possible claims.

FOGC took leases on the Nonconformist Chapel and the Gatehouse in order to protect them from inappropriate development. FOGC had always planned to restore these buildings and put them to use for the benefit of the Cemetery and the local community. The Council began to work positively with the Friends and in 1998 a Council Committee agreed in principle that FOGC could submit a bid for the development of the site to the Heritage Lottery Fund. The bid was successful and the Friends were able to rebuild and refurbish the Gatehouse area. This provided the Friends, which in 2005 became the Sheffield General

Cemetery Trust (SGCT), with offices of its own at one side and a source of income from the rental of a flat on the other.

The Gatehouse from Cemetery Avenue

An application to the Architectural Heritage Fund's "Challenge Fund" for a capital grant to repair and fit out the Nonconformist Chapel was unveiled jointly in 2013 by members of the Trust, Sheffield City Council and the South Yorkshire Buildings Preservation Trust. The plan was to carry out repairs to the Chapel, reinstate windows, install heating, lighting, disabled access, plus toilet and kitchen facilities in order to bring it back into use. It was hoped to use the building for educational, arts and cultural events as well as making it available for private hire.

The application was successful and additional funding was awarded by Waste Recycling Environment Ltd. under their Heritage Fund programme together with a contribution from Sheffield City Council. The restoration, repair and fit-out of the Chapel started in March 2014 with the digging of a service trench to connect the Chapel to the

Gatehouse. The repair and restoration of the Chapel followed and by September 2015 visitors were able to access the Chapel to see the extensive restoration. Gone were the bricked-up windows and gloomy interior: instead, the delicately latticed original window framework had been exposed and restored to let the light stream into the large and airy building. Fundraising to equip the Chapel continued but the work already carried out had enabled the building to be removed from the English Heritage "At Risk" register. Underfloor heating and a new stone floor were laid before the restoration of the Chapel was successfully completed and reopened in November 2016 as the Samuel Worth Chapel.

After its renovation the Chapel became used for exhibitions, community events, music and drama performances and concerts, private parties, conferences and corporate away days. The Chapel is a valuable source of income for the Trust, particularly since becoming a wedding venue and gaining a licence to host events throughout the year.

The Samuel Worth Chapel

The Commonwealth War Graves Commission (CWGC) screen wall commemorates the men and women buried in the Cemetery who died as a result of the First and Second World Wars. When the Memorial was originally commissioned it was sited at Sheffield's City Road Cemetery. The General Cemetery was not thought to be a suitable location because it was such an area of neglect. Due to the tremendous work done by volunteers in improving the landscape over the last 20 or more years the CWGC decided that the Memorial should be placed near to the graves of the men and women it honours. It was re-sited at the General Cemetery in 2015.

The War Memorial

The lower wall of the Catacombs collapsed early in 2013 and another longer section bulged dangerously. The unsafe structures were supported with timber shoring and fenced off for the safety of the public. By 2018 the Cemetery was on Historic England's "Heritage at Risk Register" due to the significant levels of structural repair required to conserve the complicated tiers of retaining walls that were largely unseen but intrinsic to the Cemetery's design. Some had not had significant repair work since being built. A bid was made by Sheffield City Council for funding to conserve and improve the Cemetery with plans including work on listed and non-listed historic features: walls, Catacombs, monuments, improvements to site entrance points, landscape improvements including signage, management of trees and vegetation, lighting and car parking.

£3 million was awarded by the Parks for People programme, a joint initiative between the National Lottery Heritage Fund and the National Lottery Community Fund. With £800,000 added by Sheffield City Council, the proposed repair and conservation work including a three-year activity programme was made possible. Work started in November 2021 with contractors moving on site to start a 15-month programme of work. The most dramatic change was to the Catacombs where the concrete balustrade and the raised area by the main drive were carefully removed without disturbing any burials and the levels restored to those of the original 1836 design. One section at the west end was left and marked with the date 1937 to demonstrate that period in the site's history. The whole structure was stabilised with hidden steel reinforcements and rebuilt in part, with new balusters where necessary.

In 2023 after the contractors' work was complete, Historic England removed the Cemetery from the Heritage at Risk Register.

The restored Catacombs

1937 date stone

Above the Catacombs

Repairs were made to Stalker Walk, the Chapel retaining wall, the Cemetery Road boundary wall and the Chapel steps. The headstones placed on the top of the Catacombs in the 1980's clearance of the Anglican area were relocated, either alongside the main drive or back into the Anglican area. At all times efforts were made to reuse material found on site: stone edging, steps and abandoned, damaged headstones lacking inscriptions were reused. The path running up from the side of the Nicholson monument to just below the Cemetery Office was sympathetically restored to its original form with evenly laid stones and new coping on the wall. Sadly, one of the stonemasons, Andy Smith, died after completing this work; the path remaining as a memorial to him.

Memorial to Andy Smith[7]

Work around the Samuel Worth Chapel saw improvements to the setting and access to the Chapel by the installation of an electricity supply for new lights, better drainage and path surface improvements before the contractors left the site in May 2023.

Restoring the Landscape

Following Chris Brooks' report to English Heritage in 1994 in which he cited the Cemetery as one of national significance and a report on Sheffield's parks by landscape historian Joan Sewell commissioned by Sheffield Council, the site gained national recognition by English Heritage. In 1998 it was included in the National Register of Parks and Gardens of Historic Interest at Grade II. This was upgraded in 2009 to Grade II*, important because only 5 per cent of England's heritage is listed at Grade II* or above. In 2000 the section of the Porter Brook at the base of the Cemetery also became a designated Conservation Area.

The Doorstep Green's policy of the Countryside Agency provided a funding opportunity for further landscape improvements in 2004. The Environmental Consultancy of the University of Sheffield (ECUS), working in liaison with the Cemetery Trust and English Heritage, designed and supervised a scheme to enhance the existing planting and provide new seating areas and paths with a view to encouraging more public use of the site.

The Memorial Garden was established near the Gatehouse with low maintenance ornamental planting and in 2004 the site was designated a Local Nature Reserve and a Local Wildlife Site.

Paths were carefully laid out to reinstate those of the original Marnock plan. As a design feature at the end of the restored Marnock path, 29 large quarried blocks of stone demonstrating different rock types were arranged in a large spiral designed by Adrian Hallam. The project was instigated by Peter Kennett with a grant provided by the Curry Fund of the Geologists' Association.

Entrance to the Memorial Garden

The Geological Stone Spiral

The Cemetery landscape is maintained by a dedicated team of landscape volunteers. When the Cemetery Trust won a Bronze Rose at the Yorkshire in Bloom Awards in 2011 the restoration and revitalisation of the site was described by the judges as "one of the mightiest tasks ever to be undertaken". 2015 saw a Gold Rose being awarded not only in recognition of all the work done on the landscape but also of the work done in bringing a listed building back into use for the community and the schedule of public events put on by the Trust.

The site is carefully managed and any changes respect both its listed status and wildlife value. A pond was created in 2018, a composting compound installed, and bird and bat boxes erected. Construction work as part of the Lottery funded project in 2022/23 inevitably caused some disruption but work was carried out to minimise the impact as much as possible. Small crevices for bats were left in structures that were repaired, wildflower meadows were developed and more relaxed mowing regimes implemented.

The Memorial Garden area close to the Gatehouse was rejuvenated in 2023. At that year's Royal Horticultural Society Flower Show Tatton Park one of the show gardens was designed by Sheffield landscape architect, Ollie Pike, for its sponsors, the Bible Society. Ollie's design was inspired by Psalm 27 and the Cemetery where he had spent time during the Covid lockdowns of 2020-2021, finding a place to reconnect with nature and a source of solace and spiritual comfort. When the Show closed, the Bible Society generously donated 1500 plants from the Psalm 27 Garden to the Cemetery for the benefit of the local community. The Memorial Garden was reinvigorated by the introduction of the meadow style grasses and native wildlife friendly plants with their beautiful textures and calming soft colours.

The landscape of the Cemetery remains an attractive place, well used by the public who often refer to it as "the Cemetery park". Management of the whole site is geared to creating and maintaining a variety of natural habitats so that native plant species, fungi, birds and animals can flourish. The broad open area of the cleared Anglican plots is mown grassland while paths wind through the Nonconformist area where some original planting still exists: there are old oaks, rare hollies, weeping ash and fine Oriental plane trees. The mature trees, regenerating woodland, old structures and dense areas of bramble and

The Memorial Garden
2023

other shrubs mean the Cemetery is an important refuge and stepping-stone for wildlife. The River Porter is a wildlife corridor connecting the Cemetery to the city and the wider landscape of the Porter Valley and Peak District beyond. Despite all the challenges and changes that it has faced the Cemetery can still be described as it was in *White's Gazetteer and General Directory of Sheffield* of 1837: "a delightful spot for the perambulations of the living and a safe depository for the dead". Working in conjunction with the Parks and Countryside Service of Sheffield City Council, the Trust will continue to ensure the Cemetery remains safe, secure and relevant for future generations.

Burial Plots and Monuments

The income of the Sheffield General Cemetery Company (SGCC) was in part derived from the sale of plots of land to private individuals and organisations in perpetuity. The purchaser could determine who was buried in the grave and make decisions about the stone and memorial inscription.

For those less well off, public graves were available at a much-reduced price and without a stone marker. Just under 40 per cent of all the burials in the Cemetery were in public graves. Ownership of public graves was retained by the General Cemetery Company and the graves were used to bury unrelated individuals. Interments in a public grave could continue for several years and many were in the less attractive areas near the river. Approximately 15 per cent of all the graves are public graves, that is 2,400 plots and 19 vaults in the Catacombs. Public graves were also used for pauper burials where the burial and funeral expenses were paid for by the Poor Law authorities.

Many of the public graves were used for multiple interments. The highest number of burials in a single plot was 85, 16 (six adults and ten infants) of them from the Workhouse. The rest were burials in which the occupants or their families paid the burial costs themselves but could not afford a private grave. In total there were 15 adults and 70 infants interred in the grave. The Catacombs were also used for multiple burials. Vault EE in the lower tier was used between 1924 and 1949 for 1095 burials of which 511 were stillborn babies.

Monument Design

In the early Nonconformist period of the Cemetery's history the monument designs were overwhelmingly classical in style. The headstones and monuments were largely Greek Revival which included the use of classical patterning, simple curved top gravestones and symbols such as urns, pyramids and columns. There were a significant number of obelisks from this period, echoing the overall styling of the Cemetery. It was not until the mid-nineteenth century in the consecrated area that the cross motif and pointed headstone began to appear.

The Cemetery Company soon realised that money was to be made from stone masonry. Within a year of the Cemetery's opening they resolved to employ "a skilful and ingenious Mason.....to secure the richest display of elegance, propriety and taste in the varied memorials which affection may place upon the ashes of departed friends".[8] In 1838 a stonemason's workshop was established on the site. However, there was competition from other stonemasons at work in the neighbourhood including Joseph Hadfield, Benjamin Fidler and the Eatons of Cemetery Road.

In 1849 Edwin Smith established his Marble and Stone Works on Cemetery Road out of which came some of the Cemetery's best designed and executed monuments. Theophilus Smith, son of Edwin, made a name for himself as an early documentary photographer and was also an excellent draughtsman and monumental sculptor. He had a genuine interest in the principles of Christian monument design and published several catalogues on the subject. Theophilus Smith was regarded as one of the most important monument designers at work in this period as he established a sense of private property in his elaborate and emphatic use of wrought iron railings around monuments.

With the increasing demand for gravestones, coupled with increasingly mechanised production processes, it became possible to develop gravestone templates, machine carved, which people could tailor to their wishes. Pattern books began to appear and Theophilus Smith was swift to employ this method as a way of illustrating the many designs on offer. He had his finger on the pulse of the monument market, developed monument templates and understood the new concept of commercialisation which asserted itself formally in the Great Exhibition of 1851. This trend signalled a gradual but notable decline in the standard of gravestone design for the majority. From then on there would be less hand carving and a greater uniformity of gravestones.

Sadly, Smith's personal and working life became a disaster following a carriage accident that crippled him. He became unable to work, lost his income, became an alcoholic, was charged with wife beating and died in disgrace. The General Cemetery has many examples of his work though much was removed or destroyed when part of the site was cleared in 1980.

Various Company Minutes show that the General Cemetery Company wanted to impose a financial penalty if any other masons were used in preference to the Company mason, and, indeed, they gave themselves the right to reject stones produced by others. Stones and monuments always had to be submitted for approval by the Company.

The majority of gravestones are made of Brincliffe Blue sandstone quarried locally. The stone resists weathering and retains much of its detailing so that the inscriptions can still be read decades later. The advent of the railway in the 1840s meant it was easier and cheaper to bring stone from other areas, so Italian Marble began to be imported, as well as Aberdeen Granite and Larvikite from Norway. Such materials were expensive and only used for the more prominent monuments of wealthier people. Monuments became more varied in design and the Company's Annual Reports proudly record the erection of the grander examples. In 1876 there is mention of "an elegant monument in memory of the late Dr Sale by his family at a cost of £500, surmounted by a high cross of Mansfield red stone and at the base are four symbolic figures....Also a white marble monument to Councillor Mills".

The design of the monuments and gravestones and their inscriptions give fascinating insights into the lives of the people buried in the Cemetery. Some of the more interesting structures and residents are introduced in the following pages. Four of the memorials within the site are listed Grade II structures and considered particularly distinctive and architecturally significant.

Some notable memorials

George Bassett, (1818-1886), sweet manufacturer and local politician

George Bassett was born in Ashover, Derbyshire and in 1832 began an apprenticeship to a confectioner in Chesterfield. He opened his first confectionery shop on Broad Street, Sheffield in 1841 before expanding into wholesale and opening a manufacturing venture on Portland Street in 1859. As well as his involvement in the confectionery trade, George Bassett was a well-known local figure, became a City Alderman and was elected Town Mayor in 1876.

Bassett died in 1886 and was buried close to the Cemetery's western wall, to the right of the Egyptian archway as you go up the hill. His memorial, an unimpressive rectangular block with a shield relief on the front, was originally topped with an obelisk, which now lies on the ground in front of it.

Memorial to George Bassett

Many visitors to his grave associate him with Liquorice Allsorts and Jelly Babies, sweets made under his name today. However, Bassett would not recognise these confectionery lines as they were created after his death. It was not until 1899, thirteen years after he died, that

"Liquorice Allsorts" came into being. A salesman, Charlie Thompson, presenting a tray of sweets to a shop owner, tripped and the tray of sweets fell to the floor, all mixed up. Rather than sort them out, the shop owner sold this jumble to his customers as "all sorts" and the brand was born.

George Bennet, (1775-1841), missionary, social reformer and benefactor

Memorial to George Bennet

The Bennet monument (listed Grade II) in front of the steps of the Samuel Worth Chapel is one of the most significantly sited memorials in the Cemetery. Framed by two weeping ash trees, it occupies a key vista from the Samuel Worth Chapel across the valley. It is 15 feet high and bears a relief sculpture of George Bennet leaning on a globe with a palm tree behind him representing his missions across the world.

There is a link between this monument and the Montgomery monument erected in front of the Anglican Chapel a few years later. The two men were good friends who corresponded over many years and were both campaigners against the slave trade and founders of the Sheffield Sunday School Union. Bennet went on the longest mission ever undertaken by the London Missionary Society. His journal formed the basis of the book, edited by James Montgomery - *"Journal of Voyages and Travels by the Rev. Daniel Tyerman and George Bennet, Esq"*.

Bennet died suddenly in 1841 in London and was buried in Hackney. The monument was constructed after a public subscription organised by the Sheffield Literary and Philosophical Society of which Bennet was an honorary member and the Council of the Sheffield Sunday School Union.

Thomas Burch, (1808-1865), local businessman and politician

In 1870 the imposing monument to Thomas Burch was erected by his widow in a prime position in front of the Samuel Worth Chapel. The monument was 14.5 feet tall and made up of a column on a plinth, topped by an urn, within an enclosure of elaborate wrought iron.

Under his original family name, Thomas Edward Mycock, he served for many years as an Alderman for Sheffield and took a prominent part in local affairs. He was chairman of the Watch committee, a Poor Law Guardian and director of the Water Company. He was a shrewd businessman and as a builder and contractor had a very good reputation for his workmanship, which secured him contracts for building many of the great manufactories and private residences of the better class that were then being built.

Memorial to Thomas Burch

In January 1865 as recommended and requested by the will of his late father-in-law, John Burch, Thomas, his wife Harriet, three sons and two daughters all changed their surname by Deed Poll from Mycock to Burch. He was described in his obituary as a man of "plodding industry, great natural shrewdness and an unquestionable aptitude for business, which raised him years ago to a good social position". His family were clearly intent that this position should be reflected in his memorial.

The Cole Brothers, shopkeepers and philanthropists

The three Cole brothers, John, Thomas and Skelton, were all buried in the General Cemetery. The dominant dark obelisk at the side of the path as you walk up the main drive marks John's grave and Thomas's grave was a few plots to the right. Skelton was buried near to the Egyptian archway as you go up the hill. However, the greatest memorial to the brothers was probably the store named after them which they first established on Fargate in 1847. Selling drapery, carpets and furnishings, by 1892 it had grown to four floors with 350 employees.

The brothers all died between 1896 and 1902 after lifelong service to commerce, the Methodist Society, support for the Jessop Hospital for Women, the Totley Orphanage, education and promoting abstinence from alcohol. After the death of Thomas Cole, Cole Brothers was run by the sons of Thomas and Skelton, and continued to expand and move with the times. By 1909 they were employing women, delivery vans were introduced in 1911 and cash registers in 1916. The Cole family sold the iconic store to Selfridges in 1920 and in 1939 Selfridges sold it to John Lewis. It was John Lewis who relocated the store to Barker's Pool in 1963 and the original building, on the corner of Fargate and Church Street, and known locally as Coles Corner, was sold. The much-loved department store failed to reopen when Covid restrictions were eased in 2022.

Memorial to John Cole

Mark Firth, (1819-1880), steel master, politician and philanthropist

The Firth memorial (listed Grade II) built over a vault, was constructed between 1869 and 1876 and stands at the crossroads of the main paths by the junction of the Nonconformist and Anglican areas of the cemetery. Made of Aberdeen granite, topped by a draped urn, it stands about three metres tall. The monument is in an enclosure with railings made in Firth's own Norfolk works. These substantial railings have elaborate medallion designs. There is a large slab in front of the monument covering an entrance to the vault accessed by a flight of steps. Mark Firth commissioned the monument and chose the spot for the grave, prepared for the loss of one of his daughters, Margaret Maria who died in 1869. The grave also contains other members of the Firth family. Mark Firth was a highly successful industrialist, establishing the largest steel company in Sheffield, as well as a substantial philanthropist, Mayor and Master Cutler of the town. He donated the land now known as Firth Park to the people of Sheffield and founded a technical school which formed the foundation of Sheffield University.

Memorial to Mark Firth

Margaret Green, (1824-1869), wife and mother

Margaret Green's memorial was originally sited in the Anglican area of the Cemetery but was moved during the clearances in 1980 and now lies flat on the Catacomb path. As well as Margaret, who died in 1869 aged 45 whilst undergoing breast surgery, her gravestone memorialises ten of her children who died young. This simple memorial and its inscription symbolises the plight of women in the nineteenth century – constantly having and losing children and then themselves suffering an early death. "She was brought as a lamb to slaughter, and as a sheep before her shearers is dumb, so she openeth not her mouth" is part of the inscription.

Margaret and her family lived close to an abattoir and a refuse tip and ten of her children died of diseases associated with poor living conditions such as typhoid and dysentery. Four of Margaret's children did survive into adulthood. After her death her husband Thomas remarried and had four more children with his second wife.

Memorial to Margaret Green,
in its original position

John Gunson, (1809-1886), water engineer

John Gunson's place in Sheffield's history was assured as a result of the devastating Flood that engulfed villages above Sheffield and a large part of the Don Valley in March 1864. When the Dale Dyke dam burst, unleashing millions of tons of water "with the noise of thunder, the swiftness of lightning and the force of Niagara" according to *Hunter's Hallamshire*, onto a sleeping population, over 240 people died. 66 of the Flood's victims were buried in the General Cemetery.

John Gunson had been involved in overseeing the dam's development and was the engineer responsible for checking the dam, which he did on the day of the disaster. The area had been subject to torrential rain for a prolonged period and the sodden ground eventually started to slip. John Gunson tried to avert the disaster by blowing up part of the dam wall to divert the flow of the water, but the explosives failed to ignite.

Having endured accusations of blame from a furious Coroner at the inquest, he was haunted by the disaster for the rest of his life although The Sheffield Waterworks Company supported him and continued to employ him for many years. A further committee of enquiry exonerated him in later years. His damaged chest tomb is tucked away on a side path near the Cemetery Office.

Memorial to John Gunson

Samuel Holberry, (1814-1842), Chartist

For many people one of the most important graves in the Sheffield General Cemetery is that of Samuel Holberry who died in 1842 in prison at York Castle. Though not a native of Sheffield, Holberry was a leading figure in the Chartist Movement in the area. Almost all the points included in the People's Charter that the Chartists advocated, such as universal suffrage, have now become law. In the words of his modest gravestone near the Cemetery Office in a line which includes the graves of other Chartists, what happened to him was a punishment for "advocating what to him appeared to be the true interest of the people of England".

Holberry was arrested for allegedly plotting to seize the Town Hall and a Coaching Inn and hold them against the Civil Authorities. Although not sentenced to hard labour, Holberry was illegally forced to work on the treadmill at Northallerton Prison.

Memorial to Samuel Holberry

73

He was moved to York Gaol but his health had been damaged and he died there aged 27. Following his death, he became known as a martyr for the Chartist cause and some 50,000 people followed his coffin from the railway station to the Cemetery and are said to have hung from the trees to get a better look, an event well documented in the press of the time.

The gravestone also commemorates his son Samuel, who died aged 18 weeks old while his father was in prison, but not his wife, Mary Cooper, who remained active in the Chartist movement and was also buried in the grave.

James Montgomery, (1771-1854), writer, publisher, campaigner, philanthropist

Scotsman James Montgomery, perhaps best remembered today as the writer of the hymn "Angels from the Realms of Glory", was a poet, writer, philanthropist and editor of the *Sheffield Iris*, which later became the *Sheffield Telegraph*. Like Samuel Holberry he had spent time in York Gaol for preaching sedition through the columns of the *Iris* by supporting the claims of working men for better conditions. He was also involved in the Sheffield Sunday School Union, which he had helped to establish along with George Bennet (see above).

At his death he was given a public funeral at St George's Church and the cortege bringing his body to the General Cemetery was followed by a large crowd. His body was buried in the centre of a circular enclosure surrounded by wrought iron railings, the Rotunda, outside the Anglican Chapel. In recognition of Montgomery's importance to their development, the Sheffield Sunday School Union instigated the collection of a public subscription which paid for the erection of a statue over the grave in 1861. The statue cost over £1,000, a great deal of money at that time, and much of it was said to have been raised in pennies and tuppences from children attending Sunday School classes.

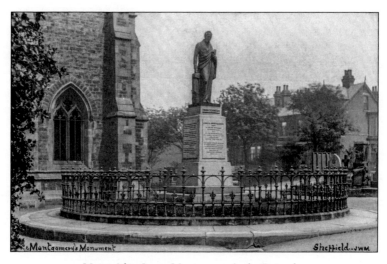

Memorial to James Montgomery in the Rotunda,
prior to its removal to Sheffield Cathedral

Unfortunately, over the years, the statue fell into disrepair and amid the uncertainty surrounding the Cemetery's future in 1971, the Sunday School Union again raised the money to have both it and Montgomery's remains removed to their present resting place at the side of Sheffield Cathedral.

James Nicholson, (1824-1909), industrialist

The Nicholson memorial (listed Grade II), one of the most beautiful in the Cemetery, dates from around 1872, although the plot had been in use by the family since 1861. It has a principal position on the main path at the central junction of the Cemetery site, located opposite the Mark Firth memorial and sits on the dividing line separating the Nonconformist and Anglican areas. It is a tall chest tomb within a triangular enclosure with a statue of a woman kneeling in prayer on top. It used to have statues of angels on each corner, but these have now gone. The monument, commissioned by Nicholson after the death of his first wife Harriet in 1872, also commemorates other members of the Nicholson family, including James himself, his second wife Katherine Sarah who died in 1923 and children from both marriages. The Nicholson family were prominent steel industrialists in Sheffield in the nineteenth century with premises in Mowbray Street.

Memorial to James Nicholson

William Parker, (1784-1837), exporter of cutlery, Nonconformist

An exporter of cutlery and a prominent Nonconformist, Parker died suddenly aged 53. He was a highly respected and "much lamented gentleman" and an estimated 1,500 people attended his funeral. After his death in 1837 his friends, the "principal merchants" of the city, raised a subscription to erect a monument in his name. A competition was held and about 30 competitors laid their designs before a committee formed by the subscribers. The design submitted by Samuel Worth was chosen of an elaborate monument (listed Grade II) evoking a design from classical antiquity. It was in the style of the Choragic monument of Lysicrates[9] in Athens and was one of only three of similar design in the entire country. Costing around £200, it was a significant addition to the early Cemetery landscape and appeared in the first engravings of the Cemetery. Situated to the west of the Samuel Worth Chapel it was a memorial and not a grave marker as Parker was buried behind the Chapel.

Memorial to William Parker

Ernest Shuttleworth, (1894-1916), soldier

Second Lieutenant Ernest Ronald Shuttleworth of the 1st/8th Battalion of the Royal Warwickshire Regiment died on the first day of the Battle of the Somme 1 July 1916 when nearly 20,000 men were killed. Ernest Shuttleworth had joined the Royal Navy when he left school at eighteen and served at Scarpa Flow but after a time he decided that life as an ordinary seaman was rather dull so he re-enlisted in the Royal Warwickshire Regiment.

He is among the many thousands of Empire, now Commonwealth, soldiers whose bodies have never been identified and have no known grave but are remembered on the imposing Thiepval War Memorial in Northern France. He is also remembered on the pink granite chest tomb belonging to his parents, Thomas and Mary Shuttleworth, which is on the right of the path from the Egyptian Gate down to the Anglican Chapel.

Ernest's father was tormented by the fact that no body was ever found. The description "missing, believed killed" gave the cruel hope that his son was not dead and he spent the rest of his life searching for him before dying in 1922. One of the causes of death on Thomas' death certificate was "exhaustion".

Memorial to Ernest Shuttleworth

References

1. *Gazetteer and General Directory of Sheffield,* William White, 1837
2. While there are differences between Nonconformists and Dissenters their attitudes to burial places were broadly similar and the two terms have similar meanings in this book.
3. The Cholera Burial register recorded the names of the interred; only the then Master Cutler was named on the Monument.
4. Sheffield General Cemetery Company (SGCC) Minutes
5. SGCC Minutes
6. *The Sheffield Star,* 12 April 1978
7. HIC VIVIT: HE LIVES HERE
8. SGCC Minutes
9. The Choragic Monument of Lysicrates near the Acropolis of Athens was erected by the choregos Lysicrates, a wealthy patron of musical performances.

Sources

Brooks, Chris, *Mortal Remains*, Wheaton, 1989

Bailey, Brian, *Churchyards of England and Wales*, Magna Books, 1987

Curl, James Stevens, *The Victorian Celebration of Death*, Sutton Publishing, 2004

Hansard, Commons Debate, 11 April 1978, vol.947, cc1255 – 74

Harman, Ruth, Minnis, John, *Sheffield – Pevsner Architectural Guide*, Yale University Press, 2004

Horton, Jane, *Remote and Undisturbed,* 2001

Llewellyn, Nigel, *The Art of Death,* Victoria and Albert Museum, 1992

Death in England, Manchester University Press, 1999

Elliott, Brent, *Victorian Gardens*, Batsford, 1986

Loudon, J.C, *On the laying out, planting, and managing of cemeteries*, 1843, Published in facsimile with an introduction by James Stevens Curl, Ivelet Books, 1981

Meredith, Jo, *Remote and Undisturbed, Second Edition,* SGCT, 2014

Sheffield General Cemetery Trust, *The General Cemetery Company - Extracts from the Company Minutes 1834- 1949*, 2020

Smith, James, *Report on the condition of the Town of Sheffield*, The Royal Commission on the Health of Towns, 1843

Tweedale, Geoffrey, *Memorialists of the Dead: Edwin and Theophilus Smith of Cemetery Road, Sheffield,* Lulu.com, 2019

Wilson, Nyra M, *William Flockton – young man in a hurry*, Sheffield Art Review 2005

Image Credits

www.picturesheffield.com

Page 15:	Thomas Asline Ward, Master Cutler 1816, s08265
Page 19:	Obelisks belonging to the General Cemetery, Cemetery Avenue, s14218
Page 27:	Lithograph from T C Hofland's painting of Sheffield General Cemetery, s01405
Page 32:	Engraving of the Sheffield New Cemetery Church, c1848, u04972
Page 41:	Church of England Mortuary Chapel, 12 December 1940, s01094
Page 43:	The Cemetery, 1964, s01406
Page 43:	The Cemetery, 1964, s01407
Page 44:	The Cemetery, 1975, s01411
Page 44:	The Cemetery, 1975, s01412
Page 75:	Memorial to James Montgomery, s07704

Jane Horton Front cover

Andrew Littlewood

Page 25:	The Egyptian Gate
Page 50:	The Gatehouse from Cemetery Avenue
Page 54:	The restored Catacombs
Page 55:	1937 date stone
Page 56:	Memorial to Andy Smith
Page 60:	The Memorial Garden, 2023
Page 65:	Memorial to George Bassett

Kevin Pearce

Page 23:	Artist's impression of the rear of the Nonconformist Chapel

National Library of Scotland

Page 33:	1851 Ordnance Survey map
Page 36:	1894 Ordnance Survey map

Sheffield Local Studies Library

Page 34:	*Gazetteer and General Directory of Sheffield*, William White, 1852

Liam Rimmington

Page 55:	Above the Catacombs

The remaining images are from SGCT's collection.

Utmost efforts have been made to ensure copyright compliance.

Sheffield General
Cemetery Trust

SHEFFIELD GENERAL CEMETERY TRUST

In 1989 a group of local residents formed the Friends of the General Cemetery, a voluntary organisation which grew to become the Sheffield General Cemetery Trust, a registered charity (no. 1103158), dedicated to promoting and restoring the site and to protecting it as a heritage park and haven for wildlife.

As well as carrying out conservation work to maintain and enhance the Grade II* Listed landscape with its gardens and monuments, the Trust organises events and tours for the public, schools and community groups. Volunteers research the history of the site and the people buried here and produce the many books and booklets which are available to purchase. The Trust have restored the Samuel Worth Chapel and the Gatehouse (both Grade II* listed buildings) and the Chapel is now an attractive venue available to hire and licensed for events and weddings.

To continue our work we rely on volunteers, donations and members' subscriptions. You can enrol as a member and receive the regular newsletters through the SGCT website which also contains a wealth of information about the Cemetery and its residents as well as listing all the events taking place. Our aim is to encourage everyone to enjoy this historical site by walking its paths, learning its history or simply using it as a quiet place to sit and contemplate.

Visit our website www.gencem.org to find out more about the Cemetery.

"For the Living and the Dead" is one of a number of books written by volunteers at the Sheffield General Cemetery Trust which can be purchased through our website at www.gencem.org.

Canvas of Memories

Read the stories of the artists who contributed to the growth of Sheffield. They were inspired by the town and its surrounding countryside to produce art which is still inspiring us today. **Price £8.99**

A Woman's Place

Fascinating stories of Sheffield's Victorian women, some of whom fell prey to the perils of widowhood, disease, childbirth and alcoholism, but there were also those who paved the way for the opportunities we enjoy today.

Price £7.99

Sweet Remembrance

The hidden and often secret stories behind graves in the General Cemetery give a fascinating insight into our confectionery past. This book tells many of those stories and explains how they relate to the development of the UK confectionery industry. **Price £17.99**

Murder and Mishap

Over forty tales of unexpected and tragic deaths in Victorian Sheffield featuring gruesome murders, bolting horses, families lost in the Dale Dyke Flood, illegal prize fighting and drunken disasters!

Price £7.95